BELLY RUBBINS
FOR
BUBBINS

THE STORY OF A RESCUE DOG

WRITTEN BY

JASON KRAUS

ILLUSTRATION & DESIGN BY

CONNOR DeHAAN

BUBBINS BOOK CHALLENGE
Using the hashtags
#BUBBINSBOOK & #BELIEVELIKEBUBBINS
Post a picture of your rescue dog and tell their story

There once was a puppy named

Bubbins,

all he wanted was Belly Rubbins.

He grew up in a house where

his owners were mean,

he barely ate

and was never kept clean.

Bubbins did **tricks,** never barked, and he behaved each day, but when he'd roll over for Belly Rubbins, they'd shoo him away.

But Bubbins always believed and continued to say,
I'm going to get a loving family one day.

"To the corner,"

they said, where he sat quiet and
sad, no one rubbing his belly
though he hadn't been bad.

Bubbins laid on the hard
floor, and he cried and
cried, until his owner
pointed and yelled,

"get outside!"

But Bubbins always believed and continued to say,
I'm going to get a loving family one day.

Outside in the yard, and behind a tall fence,

he had many tough experiences,
which to him, didn't make sense.

BEWARE

Bubbins lived outside for

nearly 10 years,

but somehow stayed loving,

despite his fears.

Every day he told himself that he would be okay,
even in these hard times,

he would find a way to play.

But Bubbins always believed and continued to say,
I'm going to get a loving family one day.

Lonely and forgotten was the 10-year-old Bubbins,

no one to love him or give him
Belly Rubbins.

But Bubbins always believed and continued to say,

I'm going to get a loving family one day.

One sunny morning Bubbins awoke to find his
gate left open, he'd never been outside the yard,
but his spirit was unbroken.

He barked "adios"

to the only place he had ever known, smiling wide, he
peed on the fence and was free to roam.

Walking down the street,
people to the left and the right,

a nice man saw Bubbins and decided to treat him right.

"Hey there little buddy, you've got no parents or collar, I'm gonna take you to the shelter, so please don't holler."

Bubbins jumped into the big green truck and
the nice man drove away, he said,

"I'm taking you somewhere you might
get a loving family one day."

At the shelter a very thankful Bubbins lived for nearly a
year. People passing by the proud old dog, with Bubbins

shedding only a tear.

But Bubbins always believed and continued to say,
I'm going to get a loving family one day.

Bubbins never gave up, and one day a
young couple appeared,

**a woman with a friendly smile and a
big man with a beard.**

The woman turned to the man and said with a sigh,

"I can't help but feel bad for this poor little guy."

"He's been through so much, and still... look at that happy face. He deserves a home, let's get him out of this place!"

Bubbins jumped to his feet as the door swung open,
tail wagging so fast,

he was finally chosen.

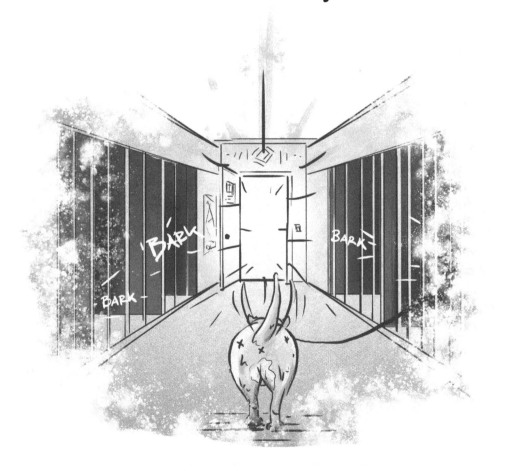

He knew deep down in his heart that he was finally okay,
because he'd been adopted by a loving family today!

As he left the shelter, he thought of all his pals, they all deserved homes, even the ones with the

scowls.

As he looked back at the shelter, he saw
all the volunteers gathered, Bubbins
loved them so much because

they showed him his life
mattered.

Bubbins tongue flapped out the window the entire ride,

the man and woman smiled and looked on with great pride.

Arriving at his new home, Bubbins ran through the door, the first thing he saw were many

new toys on the floor.

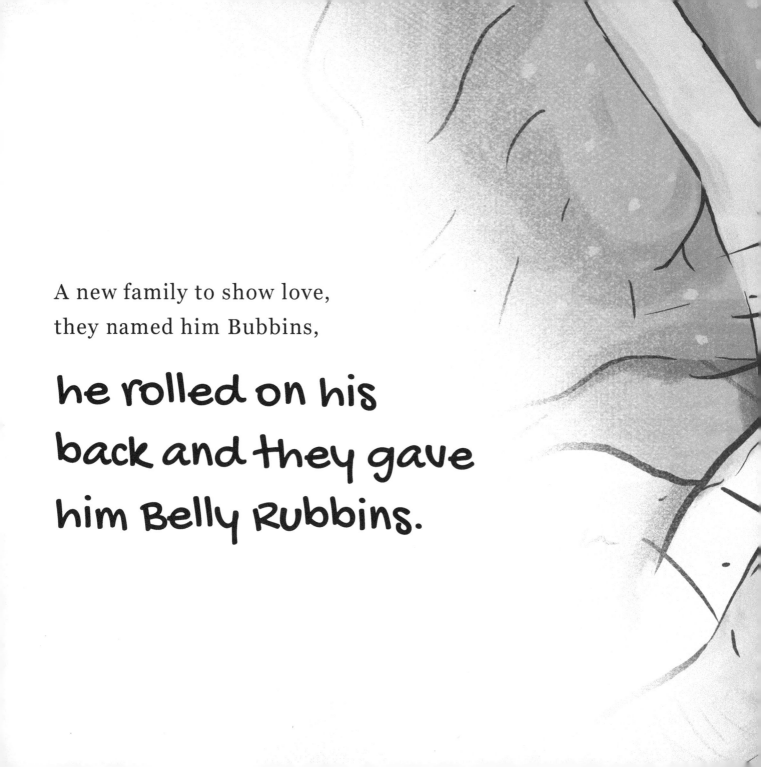

A new family to show love,
they named him Bubbins,

he rolled on his
back and they gave
him Belly Rubbins.

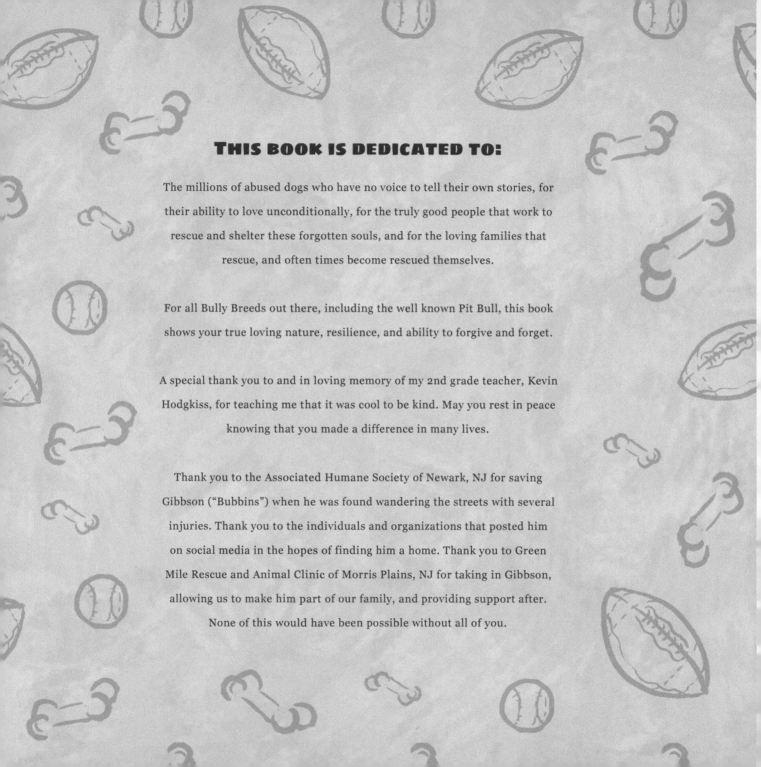

THIS BOOK IS DEDICATED TO:

The millions of abused dogs who have no voice to tell their own stories, for their ability to love unconditionally, for the truly good people that work to rescue and shelter these forgotten souls, and for the loving families that rescue, and often times become rescued themselves.

For all Bully Breeds out there, including the well known Pit Bull, this book shows your true loving nature, resilience, and ability to forgive and forget.

A special thank you to and in loving memory of my 2nd grade teacher, Kevin Hodgkiss, for teaching me that it was cool to be kind. May you rest in peace knowing that you made a difference in many lives.

Thank you to the Associated Humane Society of Newark, NJ for saving Gibbson ("Bubbins") when he was found wandering the streets with several injuries. Thank you to the individuals and organizations that posted him on social media in the hopes of finding him a home. Thank you to Green Mile Rescue and Animal Clinic of Morris Plains, NJ for taking in Gibbson, allowing us to make him part of our family, and providing support after. None of this would have been possible without all of you.

THEN

NOW

PHOTO CREDIT: IG - @MATT.JADRO

ORIGINAL STORY BY JASON KRAUS.

ILLUSTRATION AND DESIGN BY CONNOR DEHAAN.

CPSIA information can be obtained
at www.ICGtesting.com
Printed in the USA
BVHW021748050519
547409BV00012B/26/P